A Crabtree Branches Book

Today's Stars

KATE MIDDLETON

Ellen Rodger

Crabtree Publishing
crabtreebooks.com

School-to-Home Support for Caregivers and Teachers

This high-interest book is designed to motivate striving students with engaging topics while building fluency, vocabulary, and an interest in reading. Here are a few questions and activities to help the reader build upon his or her comprehension skills.

Before Reading:

- *What do I think this book is about?*
- *What do I know about this topic?*
- *What do I want to learn about this topic?*
- *Why am I reading this book?*

During Reading:

- *I wonder why...*
- *I'm curious to know...*
- *How is this like something I already know?*
- *What have I learned so far?*

After Reading:

- *What was the author trying to teach me?*
- *What are some details?*
- *How did the photographs and captions help me understand more?*
- *Read the book again and look for the vocabulary words.*
- *What questions do I still have?*

Extension Activities:

- *What was your favorite part of the book? Write a paragraph on it.*
- *Draw a picture of your favorite thing you learned from the book.*

TABLE OF CONTENTS

MODERN PRINCESS

From **commoner** to princess sounds like a fairy tale. But it is a real-life story for Catherine "Kate" Middleton.

Kate became part of the British ***Royal Family*** *when she married Prince William in 2011.*

Kate grew up in an **upper-middle-class** British home. She went to school, fell in love, and married a prince! Today she is known as Her Royal Highness The Princess of Wales.

Since her marriage in 2011, Kate has had a number of royal titles, including Duchess of Cambridge and Countess of Strathearn.

Kate is a wife, mother, and member of the United Kingdom's Royal Family. As one of the most famous women in the world, Kate's every move is followed by the **media**.

Kate's job is to ***represent*** *the British Royal Family.*

Fun Facts

Kate met Prince William, King Charles III's son, while they attended the same university.

YOUNG KATE

Catherine Elizabeth Middleton was born on January 9, 1982, in Reading, England. She grew up mostly in Berkshire, England, with her parents, Michael and Carole Middleton. She has two younger **siblings**, Philippa (Pippa) and James.

Kate has always had a close relationship with her parents.

Kate's parents worked for an airline before founding a party-supply business. Kate went to private schools where she was known to be shy and well-mannered.

Kate's parents met while working for British Airways. They started their party-supply business, Party Pieces, in 1987.

Young Kate was a good student in school, and she loved to play sports. She was captain of the girls' field hockey team. She also competed in swimming events.

Fun Facts

Kate's childhood nickname was Squeak—after Pip and Squeak, her school's pet guinea pigs. Her sister Pippa was known as Pip.

MEETING THE PRINCE

After high school, Kate took a year to figure out what she wanted to do. She joined a youth organization and traveled to Chile. She studied art in Florence, Italy. She even worked as a deckhand on a ship!

Florence is home to some of the world's greatest art and architecture.

Kate decided to study art history at the University of St Andrews in Scotland. This was the same university Prince William attended.

Founded in the 15th century, St Andrews is the oldest university in Scotland.

Kate took part in a charity fashion show at St Andrews in 2002. William noticed her and the two became friends. Later, they shared an apartment with other friends. The couple began dating in 2003 and were **engaged** in 2010.

The dress that Kate wore in the charity fashion show was sold in 2011 to a collector for around $125,000.

Fun Facts

William gave Kate a diamond and sapphire engagement ring. It was originally the engagement ring of his mother, Princess Diana.

ROYAL COUPLE

On April 29, 2011, Kate became part of the Royal Family when she married William. The London church they were married in is called Westminster Abbey. It was built in the 13th century.

After taking lessons from a professional, Kate did her own makeup for her wedding!

The royal wedding of William and Kate was watched by more than 300 million people around the world. There were around 1,900 people on the guest list, including members of royal families from all over the world.

People lined the streets to get a glimpse of the new royal couple as they made their way from the Abbey in a horse-drawn carriage.

On their wedding day, William and Kate were given new titles as the Duke and Duchess of Cambridge. Kate's new life as a royal meant she would work for the Royal Family. She had previously worked for her own family's business.

After the wedding, the Royal Family made an appearance on the balcony of Buckingham Palace.

Working members of the Royal Family support the monarch in their duties. These include attending events and giving speeches. King Charles III is the current monarch, or king. His mother, Elizabeth II, was queen when Kate married William.

Kate is known for being friendly and down-to-Earth at public events.

Kate lives with William at Adelaide Cottage, a house on the grounds of Windsor Castle.

The Prince and Princess of Wales have several places where they live. These are called royal residences, and include Kensington Palace and Balmoral Castle.

Fun Facts

Scuba diving and photography are two hobbies Kate loves. She often takes official photos of the Royal Family.

Kate and William have three children. Prince George was born in 2013. He is second in line to the British throne. Princess Charlotte was born in 2015, and Prince Louis in 2018.

The royal children sometimes attend public events with their parents and grandfather, the king.

Kate is a hands-on mom. She attends her children's sports events and school activities. Kate teaches them what it means to be a royal and encourages them to be patient and kind.

It is important to Kate that her children's lives be as normal as possible, despite their royal roles.

THE KATE EFFECT

As a royal, Kate is photographed by the media all the time. She is known for her fashion sense and her ability to make people feel at ease. Kate is a **patron** of many charities and organizations, including hospitals and groups that help children.

The **influence** Kate has over the public is known as "the Kate effect." In fact, she was chosen as one of the 25 most influential women in the UK in 2021.

Women love Kate's simple and **elegant** style. The clothing brands she is photographed in often sell out of stores!

In 2024, Kate was diagnosed with cancer. She took an almost year-long break from her work and had medical treatment for the disease. After her recovery, Kate returned to the hospital where she was treated and visited current patients.

Kate met with patients and thanked staff at the Royal Marsden Hospital, the cancer center where she received treatment.

Years before she had cancer herself, Kate **anonymously** donated 7 inches (17.8 cm) of her hair to a charity that made wigs for patients who had lost their hair.

Before she became Catherine, Princess of Wales, Kate Middleton was a sporty art history student. Kate was not born into royalty, but through her actions and style she has forever changed the British monarchy.

Fun Facts

Kate **inherited** $110 million in jewelry from Queen Elizabeth II.

GLOSSARY

anonymously (uh-NON-uh-muhs-lee): Without giving a name or identity

commoner (KOM-uh-ner): An ordinary person who has no rank or royal status

elegant (EL-i-guhnt): Tasteful or dignified in dress or style

engaged (en-GEYJD): Promised to be married

influence (IN-floo-uhns): The power to have an important effect on someone or something

inherited (in-HER-i-tid): Received from an ancestor or relative

media (MEE-dee-uh): The various means of communication, such as the Internet, TV, and newspapers, that widely reach or influence people

patron (PEY-truhn): A person who supports someone or something with money, time, or effort

represent (rep-ri-ZENT): To serve or speak on behalf of

Royal Family (ROI-uhl FAM-uh-lee): The close family of a reigning monarch, such as sons, daughters, siblings, and grandchildren

siblings (SIB-lings): Sisters or brothers

upper-middle-class (UHP-er MID-l klas): A social and economic class between the upper class and the working class

INDEX

WEBSITES TO VISIT

https://www.royal.uk/the-princess-of-wales

https://www.britannica.com/biography/Catherine-princess-of-Wales

https://www.royal.uk/the-royal-foundation-of-the-prince-and-princess-of-wales

ABOUT THE AUTHOR

Ellen Rodger won a bank-sponsored short story contest at age nine. It was the last thing her bank ever gave her for free, but it kicked-started a career in newspaper, magazine, and book publishing. Ellen has written hundreds of books for curious young people, on topics as varied as the history of the potato, urban wildlife, refugees, the Great Lakes, and explorers.

Crabtree Publishing

crabtreebooks.com 800-387-7650

Written by: Ellen Rodger
Designed by: Kathy Walsh
Series Development: James Earley
Editor: Melissa Boyce
Educational Consultant: Marie Lemke M.Ed.
Production manager: Candice Campbell

Hardcover: 978-1-0398-8036-8
Paperback: 978-1-0398-8396-3
Ebook (pdf): 978-1-0398-8156-3
Epub: 978-1-0398-8276-8

Printed in the U.S.A./CP2025

Published in Canada
Crabtree Publishing
616 Welland Ave.
St. Catharines, Ontario
L2M 5V6

Published in the United States
Crabtree Publishing
347 Fifth Ave
Suite 1402-145
New York, NY 10016

Library and Archives Canada Cataloguing in Publication
Available at Library and Archives Canada

Library of Congress Cataloging-in-Publication Data
Available at the Library of Congress

Photographs
Alamy: David Davies p 7, Maureen McLean p 8, newsphoto p 11 (left), Eddie Mulholland/Daily Telegraph p 19 (top), Grzegorz Brzeczyszczykiewiczp 23
Newscom: Doug Peters p 14, Sipa USA p 24, Polaris p 26
Shutterstock: Pete Hancock, cover, title page, p 6 (top), p 22 (bottom), p 28 (top); Mr Pics, TOC, p 4, p 29 (top); Frederic Legrand - COMEO, p 5; Wirestock Creators, p 9 (top); Todamo, p 13; Featureflash Photo Agency, p 15, p 16 (top), p 17; Thomas Dutour, p 18 (top); Shaun Jeffers, p 18; B. Lenoir, p 19 (bottom left), p 25, p 27 (top); Lorna Roberts, p 22 (top); Nigel J. Harris, p 28 (bottom); Joseph M. Arseneau, p 29 (bottom)
Wikimedia: Creative Commons, p 6 (bottom), p 11 (right), p 19 (bottom right)
All other images from Shutterstock